WHISPERING SHEETS

RINIL SRIVASTAVA

Contents

Preface

I'll name this book a magical life note book. Why? Because, this is my first poetry book and it has a magic which opemed a magical door for me that allowed me to see myself as a writer, a poet.

Like a life journal, my poetry reflects our experiences in the daily world. I believe the universe constantly speaks to us in a whisper, offers support, and asks for our assistance. Affirm the strength of time and the natural world.

Rinil Srivastava

Seven years ago, on a humid summer evening, when my internet had given up, I was revealed to an undiscovered part of me. My love for writing.

And now, seven years after that evening, I have finally published my first-ever poetry book.

Whispering Sheets is one of those works of mine for which I never had to spend hours contemplating what to write next. Each page, each poem, it wrote itself. This book would be, I believe, a mirror to almost everyone, who would be able to see some part of their life reflecting in the poems.

Antrickch Chitranshi

1. An Imperfect Beauty

Early hours of a lit summer,
Ambling down the empty road
The trees quivered cautiously,
Streetlights awfully glowed
Oh, wait! Someone's here,
A lost friend – the draughty breeze
'Here for the day's greatness.'
She greeted with a wheeze

The moon's also here
Gleaming, and upbraiding me
'How dare you stand in silence?
And not shout in glee'

Synonym to perfection
Calmest of a sight
Precious of a feeling
On an amiable summer night

And now, as I sank in tranquillity
The night's making a fall
A smoke of cigarette intruded on me,
And broke it all

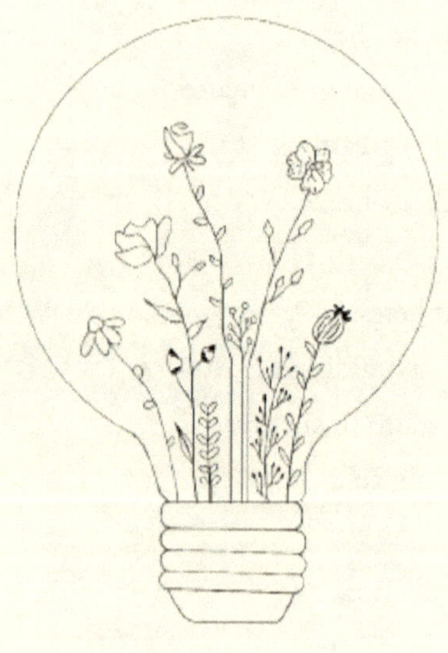

"Sometimes, not fighting a battle can also lead to victory."

2. A Phase Of Life

Occasionally, the last
do not feel like last
It unfolds,
with the days go by
the touch, the warmth of his hands,
our giggle & how the eyes connect
You get aware of it
as time moves by
Things wound up
becoming a labyrinth
happens
throughout one's phase of life.

"Profound thinking takes you to the end, beyond end."

3. Sermons Of the Cold Night

Roaming across the streets
Brought me to discover that
The cold and white snow
Doesn't suit on a rag

And another truth I found,
In the early hours
Luxury lies in the eyes
And not in the pearly showers

And so my penurious eyes
Searched over a wall of wire
My feet feathered by seeing – at a distance
The blurred shadow of a fire

Then I spent my complete warmth
in chasing that only hope
But my heart crashed when found
The masquerade was just a smoke

I learnt my third lesson
As I collapsed then and there

Expectations, but not from yourself
Bring despair in despair

I shivered on the ground
In my cold attire
Cursed breathlessly
At the one who took my fire

Just then, something called my attention
While I was struggling with winter's feud
I beheld it in disbelief –
The powdered tip of a tiny wood

In only a moment's fraction,
I could now see through it all
Acknowledged the last sermon
Of this journey, since the nightfall :

He never stole the fire
For me, he played a trick
He saved the woods from dying
And left a matchstick

"Breaking down, often gives birth to new glory."

4. Pluviophile

Meandering slowly
same as the rain, that day
Trees' leaves waggling,
Two cups on each table
at tea stall
conversing so nicely
Rain shatters the stillness
I'm
walking towards the shed
Oops! Got a light dampness
Standing beneath the shed
the dark green foliage
hidden in the woods
sparked my curiosity
Emptiness
while wandering along
the wet polished roads
hearts full, though

"*Imagining is itself an art & hence we all are an artist.*"

5. The Cycle of Nature

It arrived as gloomy news to my eyes,
In just a blink
How the enthralling sight of
maples were replaced,
by the view of the dry and tawny
woods
Yet,
I wouldn't lament or despise it.
for I know the nature of the nature;
It gives you different seasons
with differing scents
However,
one does indeed need to know
the luxurious maples
and the shedding of the last leaf
one does need both of them
– to stay, and grow, eternally

"Admiration doesn't come planned, it comes with the flow"

6. Illusion

Atop my terrace
strolling
while gazing up at the stars
A nature,
while we look at something
our minds often start wondering
Oh! The grey matter simply works in that
way.
I'm
in awe of
how light may spring from obscurity
felt,
darkness makes the value of light
more apparent.

"Most often the things we are most intimidated by are not scary, but are only new"

7. The Two of Us

It's such a peculiar place
Where life has brought us now;
We are pleased to hear
what we both said
But
we keep thinking
what we didn't

"The initial connection, the subsequent discourse and the eventual separation always occurs abruptly."

8. The Advent of Winter

The aroma of winter
passing by
within the balcony,
softens my mind.
Whispered,
Arrivals are wonderful, you know?
The chilly breeze caresses my cheeks
and
Yes! A little more
The cold air
warmed my soul,
and the world
dimming in glow.

Enter Caption

"You glow differently when you have light within yourself."

9. A Connection Forever

I'm waiting for the day
When unknowingly,
We'll run into each other.
Our eyes would struggle to talk
But our heart would beat
the same
just like that other day

"*Perfection on a beauty always coexists with an impurity yet it never suffices to undermine it.*"

10. Life Of a Leaf

Ambience altering

the wintry smoke

arrives

I

at my place

stood tall

awaiting my own fall

Prior to plummeting

in my moment

watching breeze,

garden of roses and

the play park with a windy swing

From green,

I turned in yellow.

Since it was fall,

I fell

Anew as a leaf

to be born!

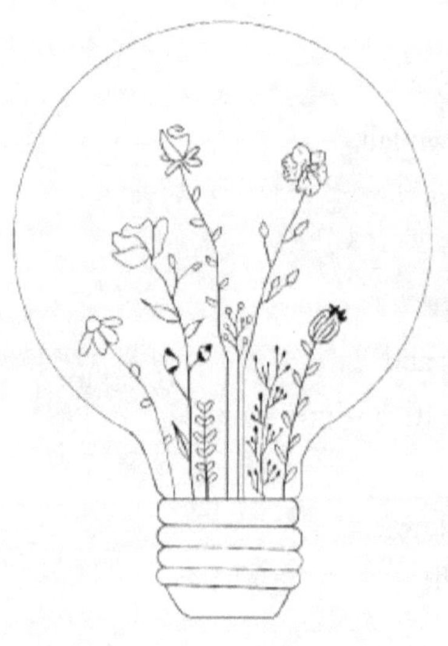

"Nature always finds a way to help us. If it didn't, we wouldn't be here."

11. An Incomplete Poem

And as I sat against the wall,
A thought made me rage:
I spent years making a key
That locked me in the cage

"In a world where everyone desires uniqueness in oneself, he only asked for a normal life."

12. A Wintry Night

Reclining on couch
with the drapes drawn
storm outside
Life at slow.
The lights flickered,
nights felt pretty, though.
In betwixt,
a honk of a car
disrupts my flow
Kindled the candles
and slurped a little water
took a book
and read a little softer.
The sound of rain
the stillness inside
drafting a poetry
wrote, "ages change, just in a glimpse…"
And oh! My eyes flickered
And I fell asleep.

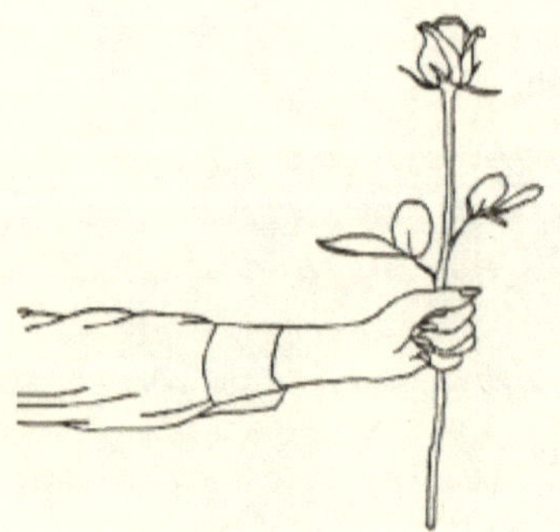

Enter Caption

"It's so enthralling to see the moon and the stars complement each other's beauty even when they are separated by miles of unfathomable distance"

13. Redemption

I stumbled upon a treasure
That got me glancing
At my hands covered with red
I cogitated,
How this could be a moment
When I could try cleaning those hands
I looked again at the treasure.
It was just a step away
And after a thought,
I stepped away

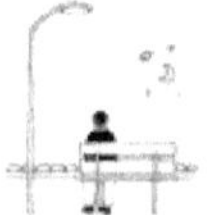

"*The relationship you have with yourself is the most important relationship in your life*"

14. Perspective

Someone said, "The only good thing happening in the world is simply that the sun rises from the east and sets in the west. One may even omit the directions here – they are worthless."

"No, the directions direct us to keep moving. Undoubtedly not the only good thing."

"The sooner you realize eyes talk,
you stop speaking"

15. I Found Him

I beheld him
from my window
wondering casually
through the chilly twilight
the hands were in the pocket
the face was benign
but,
deep in the thoughts
The flutter of butterflies
and
the chirps of the cricket
the moon began to glisten
as if,
they were complacent with the destiny
that,
I found him

"It's so enthralling to see the moon and the stars complement each other's beauty even when they are separated by miles of unfathomable distance"

16. House Is Not a home

In a gray noon
the greens look darkish
In that between
I saw an empty house
which was once a home
a cheerful home
a talkative home
A home, full of lights
A home, full of feelings
a home, full of stories
A loud thundercrack
shook my head
ran to that house
to get into the shed
Old, filthy and wretched
Nonetheless a home, full of experiences

17. Good For Yourself

If I decide one day
and try to be a king,
And turn my head away
from every rusty inn

It'd still stand upright
welcoming the coolies in need
Instead of consoling the king
their comforts it will heed

At last, the coolies will snore
In the dwellings made so cheap
And I'd still be walking like a king
But with no place to sleep

18. How Do We All Change?

Happens in one's life
things twist twice
one changes the individual
second changes the perspective
towards life.
It all depends
how you see
how you act
and have a way of life
Profoundness at each point
might take you
the higher level
doesn't matter
famously
It should be
in set of mind.

19. A Dream

In the fields of mustard
I let my thoughts stray
They move around, roam
and fall drowsy
There, they ascertained a girl
cutting and piling up
the leaves
I saw her from a mile
Oh! How lovely at noon
Someone could look
I walked towards her and made the move
She dashes to a shed as
The clouds begin to drift in
I sprinted seeing her
And got a little drenched
Just I reached the shed
She gave me a mustard leaf
Leaving as if she heard me
From a mile away
And knowing every single thing.

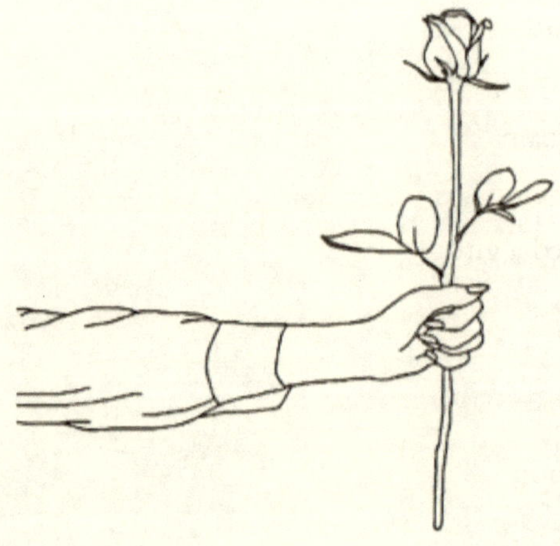

20. With You

The breeze was warm
The road's dusty
Yet,
Walking with you
In that hushed moment
Compelled my heart into
Tranquility

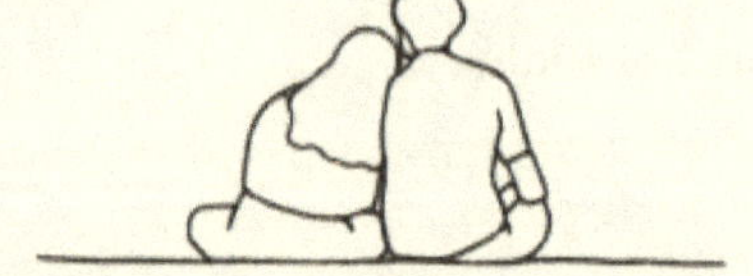